Violin

SOUNDS ON STRINGS

Maxine Alburty Madden and Harry Spencer

Illustrations by Cynthia Stuart, Nic Iacovetti Jr., and Harry Spencer

Table of Contents

Story of the Hare and the Tortoise	3.
Getting to Know Your Violin	4.
Getting to Know Your Bow	5.
The Beat	6.
Musical Symbols are like Commands	7.
Knock Knock, a rhythm song	8.
Bow and Finger Aerobics	9.
Drumming without a Drum, a rhythm duet	10.
Open String Sounds by letter names	11.
Music Symbols to make it Snappy	12.
Short and Long, open string rhythms	13.
Mix and Match Game	14.
Scales starting on open D, finger numbers	15.
"D" Scale with Boysenberry Ice Cream	16.
Mystery of the Staff	19.
Open Strings on the Staff	21.
Time Signatures	22.
Hi There! / Let's Eat Hot Dogs, open strings	23.
High Low and other open string melodies	24.
Finger Readiness on the A String	25.
Bow and Finger Aerobics II	26.
Indian Chant	27.
Slurs and a Biking Song	28.
Finding C Sharp and C Natural	29.
Key Signature: C Sharp and C Natural	30.
The Trains--any string, finger numbers	31.
Tune Snatches--finger numbers	32.
A Different "C"	33.
Stop! Look! Listen!--Key Signature	34.

Preface

"Sounds on Strings" is a readiness book to be used in the beginning weeks of instruction. It gives structure to the early stage in which much of the learning is by rote. It is a "how to read music" book and is intended as a preparation for any of the popular methods in use. However, the early pieces and "aerobics" do serve as drills and will help in building a good technique. At the same time the student is becoming accustomed to the idea of translating a symbol on the page to an action with the instrument. Written instructions are kept to a minimum to reduce clutter on the page.

By delaying the use of the staff, the material on the early pages can be used in a variety of ways. For example, below are some variations of the rhythm piece "Knock Knock Who's There?". As students achieve the skills of pizzicato, arco, and fingering, the piece could eventually be played with these sounds:

1. Clap, tap, or other percussive sound.
2. Play a key on the piano.
3. Play pizzicato on any string.
4. Play arco on the G string, then on the D string etc.
     Mark in the down-bow and up- bow signs.
5. Play all of the piece with first finger,with second finger, with third finger.
6. Using the scale, play one scale tone on each measure.
7. Class or individual composition combining various pitches with the rhythm.

You will find letter names, finger numbers, and the basic rhythms presented before the presentation of the staff. Bar lines are used to help counting. All of these non-staff pages are used while good position is being established on any string. At the same time the student is learning about notation.

The staff is introduced with the open string placement. This is followed by notation for A, B, C♮ and C♯ on the A-string.. Several little pieces serve as drills for looking at the the key signature. By the completion of this book the student will feel more comfortable with other methods and notation in general.

Acknowledgements

Most of the illustrations have been done by Cynthia Stuart and Harry Spencer. Nic Iacovetti Jr. illustrated the violin, viola and bow pictures on those pages. Piano accompaniments for "Trains", "Indian Chant" and melodies using the open string on pages 23 and 24 were written by Carolyn Mathers. Many helpful comments have been made by violinists Sue Brown of Cabrillo Community College, Betty Iacovetti of Fresno Pacific University, and Dr. David Margetts, of CSUFresno. Chuck Schroeder, music coordinator of the Fresno Unified School District, arranged time for our book to be demonstrated to FUSD music teachers and gave helpful comments from his perspective. Other string teachers who have helped considerably are: Donna Moore, cellist, of the Puallyup School District in Puallyup, Wash., violinists Janice Fleming and Gaylene Joe, and cellists Shirley Douty and Ellen Sanders of Fresno Unified School District Music Department. Our daughter-in-law, Stacey Marolf, has given us encouragement and help in the non-musical activities of putting a book together. Special thanks go to many students who have helped us to learn what works and what doesn't work. These pages have been lovingly put together for the next beginners.

AMSER
P.O.Box 5985
Fresno, CA 93755-5985

The Hare and the Tortoise

The Hare was once boasting of his speed before the other animals

"I have never yet been beaten," said he,
" When I put forth my full speed. I challenge anyone here to race with me."

The Tortoise said quietly,
"I accept your challenge."

"That is a good joke." said the Hare.
"I could dance around you all the way."

"Keep your boasting till you've beaten," answered the Tortoise. *"Shall we race?"*

So a course was fixed and a start was made. The Hare darted out of sight at once, but soon stopped and, to show his contempt for the Tortoise, lay down to have a nap.

The Tortoise plodded on and plodded on. And when the Hare awoke from his nap, he saw the Tortoise just near the winnng-post and could not run up in time to win the race.

Then said the Tortoise:
"Plodding wins the Race!" from Aesop's Fables

To win in playing and reading music: *"Be like the Tortoise. Keep trying."* Keep going over what you have learned. Practice each piece over and over until it becomes easy. **Don't give up! .... Or take a nap!**

-3-

Hare & the Tortoise

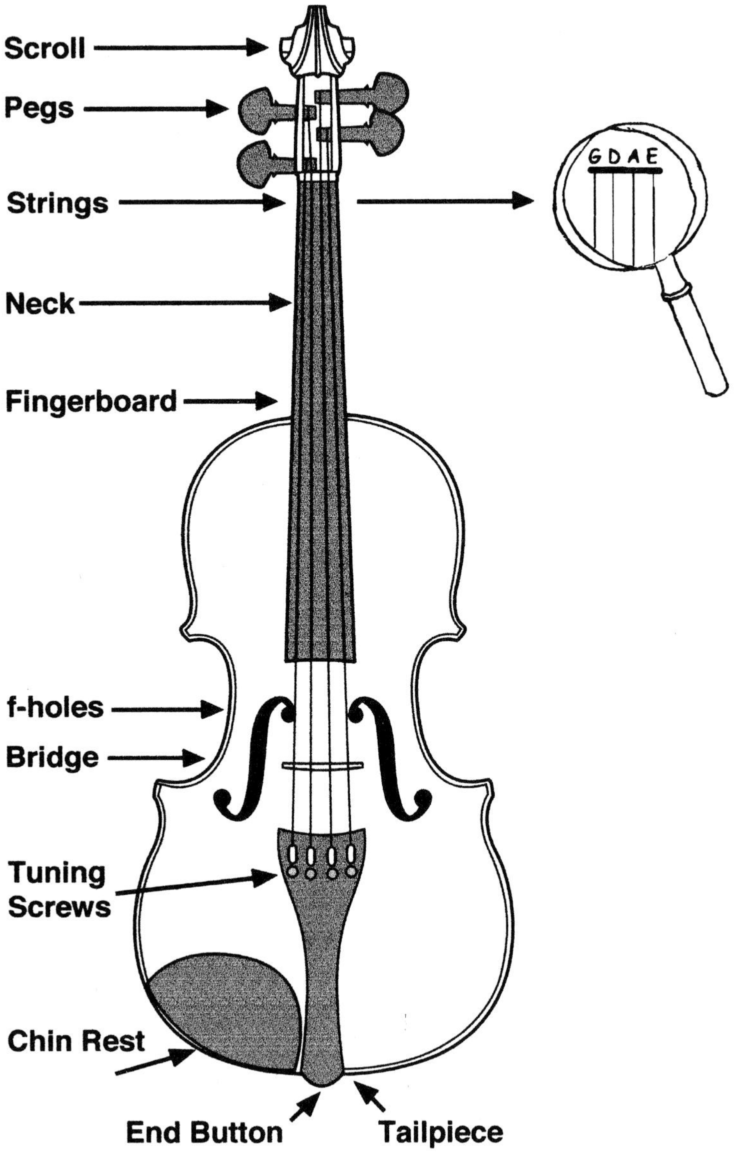
Scroll
Pegs
Strings
Neck
Fingerboard
f-holes
Bridge
Tuning Screws
Chin Rest
End Button
Tailpiece
G D A E

Getting to Know Your Violin

These items should be in your case:

Rosin - - - - - - - - -for the bow hair

Soft cloth - - - - -for wiping off dust

Pencil - - - - - - - for marking your music

Shoulder pad - - very important!

A. Your teacher will show you how to hold the violin, then:

1. Hold the violin without using your hand for a count of 20, 30, or more.
2. Pick it up 5 times and see if you can place it correctly.

B. Your teacher will show you where to place your 1st, 2nd, 3rd left hand fingers.

1. Repeat over and over: 1 . . 2 . . 3 . . 1 . . 2 . . 3 . . 1 . . 2 . . 3 . .
2. Try on each string. Be careful to place them correctly.

C. Your teacher will show you how to do "pizzicato".

Getting to Know Your Bow

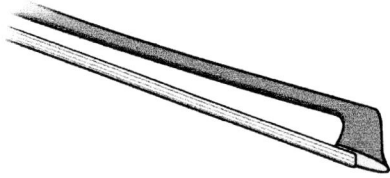

Tip

Frog

Stick

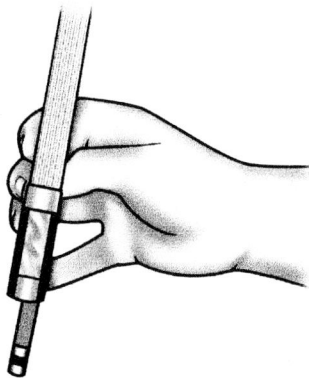

Your teacher will show you how to hold the bow, or a pencil, then try these:

1. Pick up the bow or pencil 4 times, being careful that:
   A. Tip of "pinky" sits on top of the stick.
   B. The other three fingers hang over the stick.
   C. The thumb is bent out.

2. <u>As you hold your bow or pencil</u>, try these exercises. Invent some of your own:

   A. "Elevator" --to the "top floor", then to the "basement", with the bow tip pointing to the ceiling.
   B. "Windshield Wiper" -- let your wrist and hand be the motor and your bow the wiper.
   C. Draw circles in the air or spell your name in the air.
   D. Move your arm from side to side.
   E. Reach out in front and then back to your side.

The Beat

Tap your foot so that each tap sounds steady--
like the tick-tock of a clock.

Each *"tap"* is called one beat.

When your foot comes up say, *"An'."*

That is the second half of the beat.

 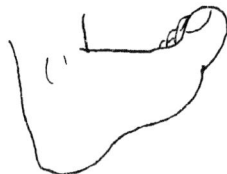  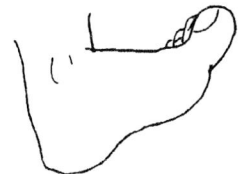

Tap   *An'*   *Tap*   *An'*

1. Say or sing "tah"
    while you tap your foot 4 Beats.

Ta - a - a - ah

2. Say or sing "tah" as a 2-beat sound or a 3-beat sound.

3. When you can say or sing and tap at the same time, study
    page 7.   Then you will be able clap the rhythm pieces
    on page 8 and 10.   "Rhythm" means a group of short
    and long sounds.

Many years ago someone decided to use symbols to stand for these sounds.
The symbol "commands" the musician to make a certain sound with a certain length.

Musical Symbols Are Like Commands

Do what I tell you!

Each of these musical symbols tells the musician what to play. It is like a command.

Three Musical Symbols

♩ = Make a sound!
   This sound must last
   for one beat of time.
   It's a quarter note!

𝄽 = Silence! Do not make a sound!
   Be <u>Quiet</u> for one beat of time!
   It's a quarter rest!

| = This line will separate the beats!
   into groups of 2, 3, 4, or more.
   It's a bar-line!

Knock Knock
Who's There?

Clap, Say "Tah", or Play Pizzicato:

Tap the air or tap your foot:

Knock, Knock!   Who's there?   Who is Knock-ing!   Who's There?

Knock! Knock!   Who's there?   Knock!   Knock!   Who's There?

Knock Knock, who's there?   Who's there?

Here's another symbol.
It means to repeat between the dotted signs.

Bow & Finger Aerobics

At first, try these with "pretend" bowing.
Later try using the bow. Keep a steady beat.

1. The Big O's

Circle Bow's

4 times on each string--all down bows ◪

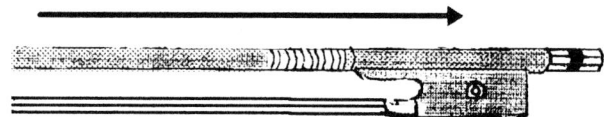

◪ ◪ ◪ ◪

4 times on each string--all up bows V

V V V V

2. The Frog/Tip Leap

| Touch the bow hair to a string at the frog. | T H E N | Touch the bow hair to the same string at the tip. | "Do this 16 times!" |

3. Robot Bow (Slow motion for crossing strings in no. 4.)

Play "D" with a down bow. . ._. . STOP the bow but keep it on the string.

Roll the bow over to the "A". . . PLAY "A" with an up bow.

Roll the bow back to the "D". . . REPEAT the motions until easy

4. Fiddler's Bow (fast and smooth string crossing)

A-E-A-E   D-A-D-A   G-D-G-D

E-A-E-A   A-D-A-D   D-G-D-G

Can you do 10 of each?

Bow-Finger Aerobics

Drumming Without A Drum

♩ = A tap or clap, or play pizzicato   ⁊ = Tap the air

Part I

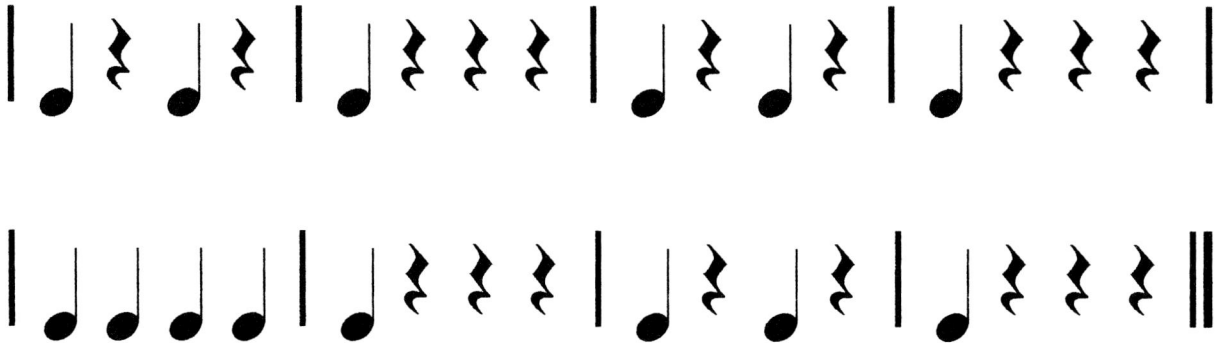

Part II

Have a friend tap Part II while you tap Part I.

Notice that you will be clapping while your friend rests.

—— Later, try playing this pizzicato or with your bow! (arco).

     Drumming without a Drum

OPEN-String Sounds

Open Strings No Fingers!

Tap your foot one beat for each letter as you play open strings:

The four strings
G D A E

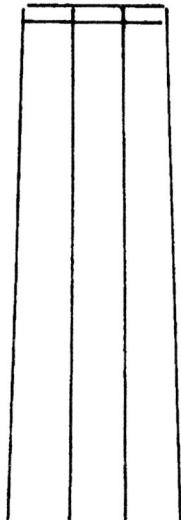

1 ‖: G G G G | D D D D | A A A A :‖

2 E E A A | D D G G | 𝄾 𝄾 G G | D D A A |

3 D D 𝄾 𝄾 | A D 𝄾 𝄾 | D G 𝄾 𝄾 | 𝄾 𝄾 E E |

4 A D A A | D D G D | A A E E | A D G 𝄾 |

Short and Long Sounds

Small letters = 1 beat sound = ♩   Large letters + —— = 2 beat sound = ♩

5 E E E— | A A A— | D D D— | G G G—

Long Long Sounds = 4 beats

6 E——— | A——— | D——— | G———

Repeat this page until it's neat and smooth!

Open String

Music Symbols: to make it Snappy!

♪ ♪ = two short sounds lasting for 1 beat.

Toot Toot

These are "eighth" notes.

Sometimes "eighth" notes are connected.

Yum Yum, Pies!

Clap, say, or play on any string with pizzicato. Later, play with the bow.

tap foot

Blue   Ber - ry,   Straw- ber - ry,   Black - ber - ry   Pie.

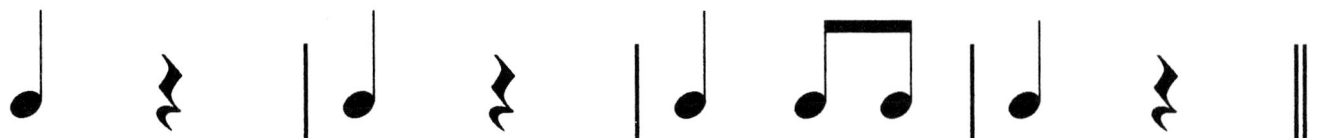

Yum!   Yum!   I   like them   all!

The Short  and Long  Notes

G

Ti Ti   Ti Ti   Ta   Ta

D

Boy-sen-ber-ry Ice Cream

A

E

Hmm! A little different!

G

Ta   Ti Ti   Ta   Ti Ti

D

Run Su-zy Run John-ny

A

E

Short and Long Notes-vn

New Symbols: ♩ = 2 beats   ♩. = 3 beats   o = 4 beats
━ = 2 beats rest   ━ = 4 beat rest

The Mix & Match Game With Open Strings

5 ways: Play across. Play down. Play up. Play diagonals. Play as you skip around.

Mix & Match

Scales

No Fingers
on the string--------

First Finger----------

Half-step

Second Finger--------
Third Finger----------

GDAE

Let's do a
"D" Scale!

This is a
whole step!

Look Out!
This is a
half-step!

Whoops!
Another
half-step!

Wow!
I made it!

2 3 2

1   1

0   0

2 3

1

0

3

2 1

0

3

2

1

0

"D"   "A"   "D"

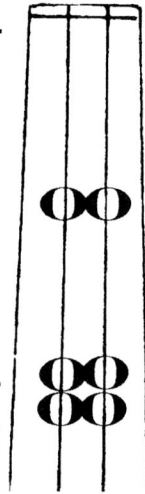

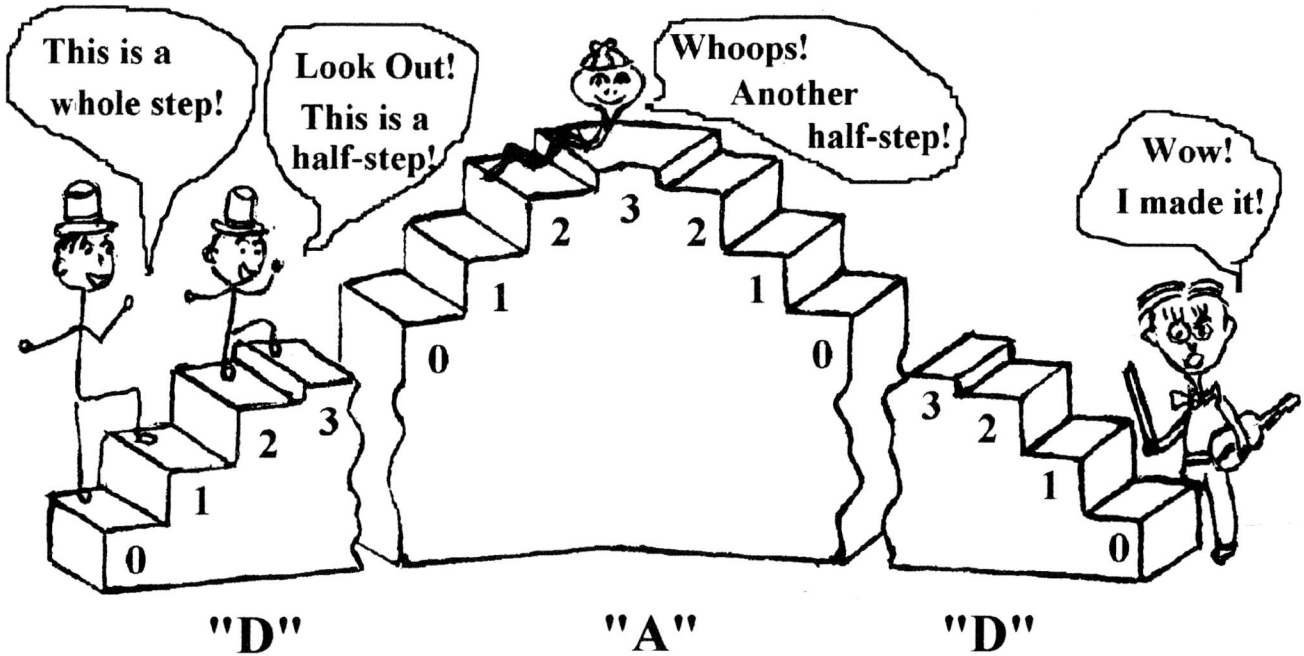

A scale is a group of 8 sounds going up and down
with steps and half-steps. Memorize the D Scale.

see page 31 and 32 for some finger-number songs.

"D" Scale Song

With Boysenberry Ice Cream

D (open string)

D-1

D-2

D-3

A (open string)

A-1 (1st finger on A)

A-2

A-3

Boysenberry Ice Cream-new

Now the scale goes   D   O   W   N

A-3

A-2

A-1

A

D-3

D-2

D-1

D

Do it again! It tastes good!

Boysen Berry Ice Cream-p2

You Have Won the Readiness Race!

You are now ready for the next race:

Reading Notes & Rhythms on a <u>Staff</u>!

The Mystery of the "Staff"

Sing a <u>high</u> squeaky sound - - - - *EEK!*

and then a <u>low</u> gravelly sound - - - - *AWK!*

To place notes for those <u>high</u> and <u>low</u> sounds
we might do something like this:

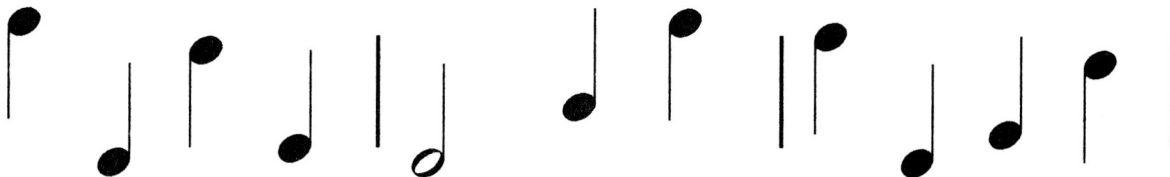

However, we don't know how
high or low
each sound will be.
<u>So!</u>

The Solution:

The Music "Staff"

5 lines   4 spaces

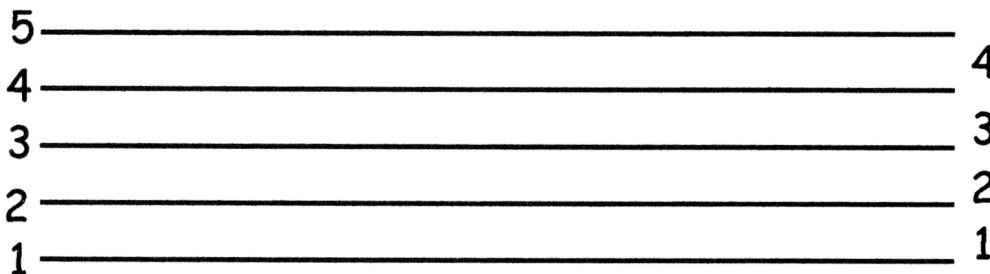

NOW for the solution

The 5 lines and 4 spaces
can show where the sounds are located on the staff.

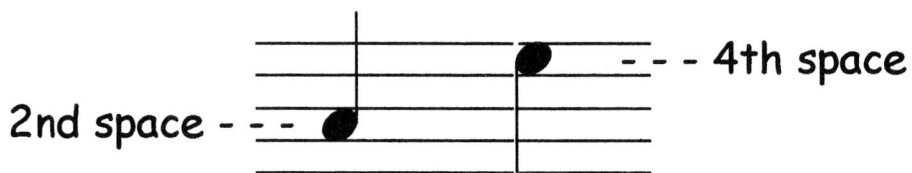

4th space

2nd space -

Play - - - - "A"   "E"
        String   String

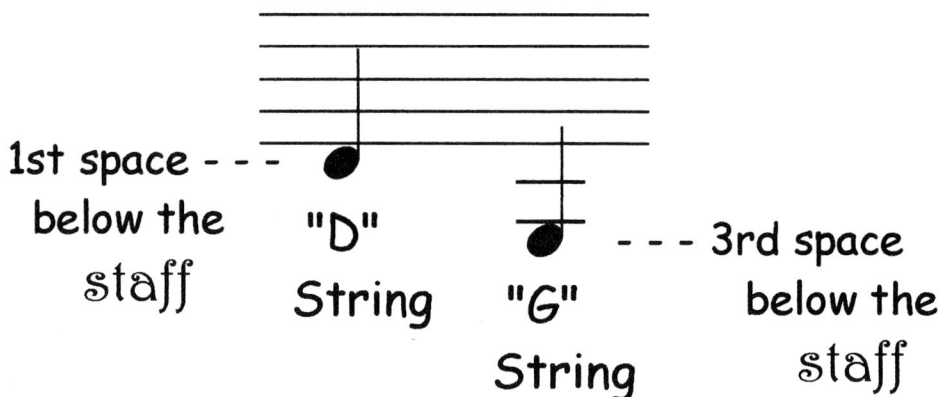

1st space - - -
below the
staff   "D"   - - - 3rd space
        String "G"   below the
              String   staff

Say these notes, then play: Draw the same notes here:

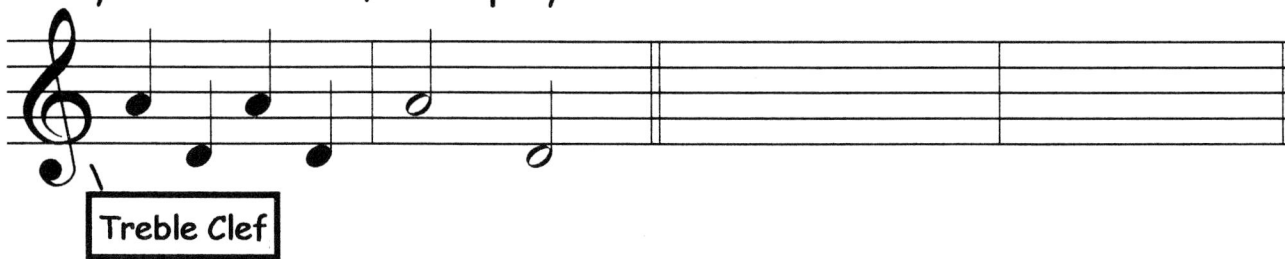

Treble Clef

The
Open
Strings

G D A E

On
The
Staff

Write the letter name under each note:

_ _ _ _ _ _ _ _ _ _ _ _ _ _ _

_ _ _ _ _ _ _ _ _ _ _ _ _ _ _

Now, Read and Play:

Gramps Likes Cauliflower

Gramps likes   cau-li-flow-er

open strings-names

Time Signatures

Clap these rhythms.

The space between the bar lines is called:

A Measure

Measures are like rooms.
Bar lines are like doorways.

With the Staff:

4/4 time is often written like this: "**C**" (common time).

> means to start the sound louder.

Time Signaatures

HI THERE! HOW DO YOU DO!

◻ move the bow to the right. This is called a <u>down-bow</u>.

∨ move the bow to the left. This is called an <u>up-bow</u>.

Hi There! How do you do!

LET'S EAT HOT DOGS NOW!

Let's eat hot dogs now!

High
Low
March

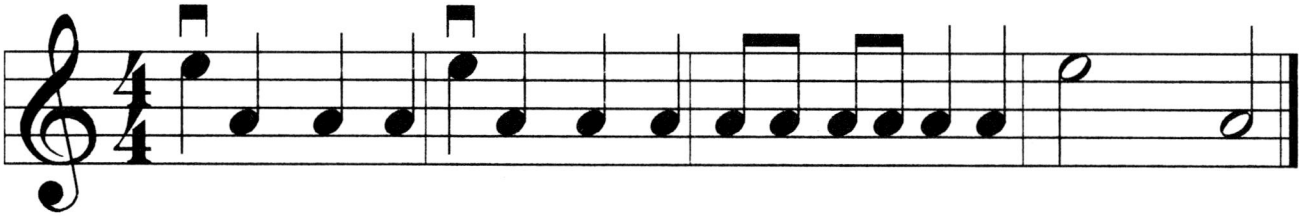

Corn
Popping

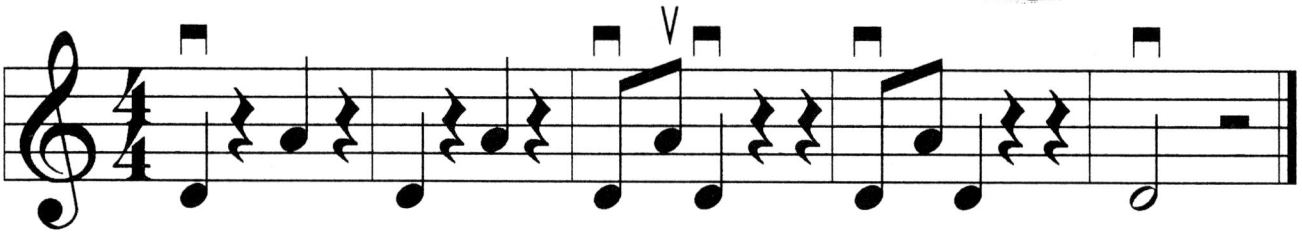

Jumping Jacks

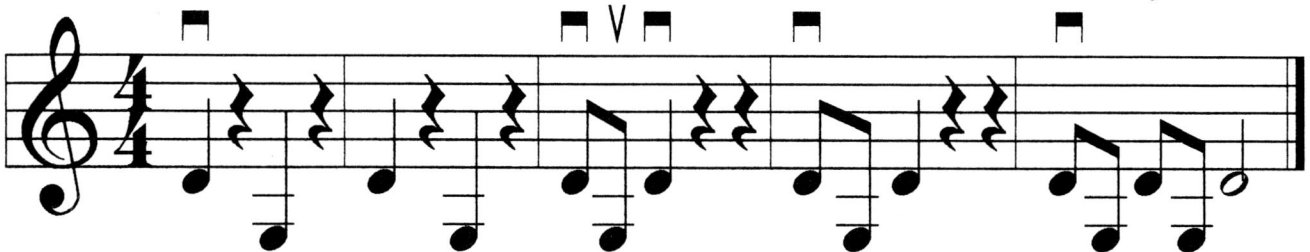

Finger Readiness on the A String

the four strings
GDAE

Beware! D will be 3rd finger on A string.

Open string	1st finger	2nd finger	3rd finger
A A A A	B B B B	C♯ C♯ C♯ C♯	D D D D
D D C♯ C♯	B B A A	A B A B	A C♯ A C♯
D D A A	C♯ C♯ A A	B B D D	C♯ C♯ D D

Now!
You can
see how the
First Finger
makes an

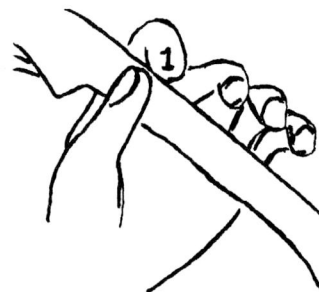

"A" into a "B"

That's what I look like.

A   B

Write in letter names:

A   B

Finger Readiness on the A String2

Bow & Finger Aerobics II

1. Double Fiddler DD--AA--DD--AA

Try on A & E then G & D. Repeat these until easy

2. Slow Drag Bow (a) Say the alphabet while you move the bow very slowly to the tip.

(b) Do the same as you move the bow back to the frog.

3. How many times can your bow "bite" the string as you play a slow drag bow?

4. Tremolo

<u>Very Fast</u> tiny bows at the tip------Do on each string.

> Now! Have some Fun! <u>Pat</u> your head and <u>Rub</u> your tummy!
>
> If you can do that, Trills, Aerobic #5, will be easy!

5. Trills (The Finger Wiggle)

A <u>slow bow</u> using (0-1-0-1-0-1-0-1) quickly many times.

Do it with these fingers, too:

1-2   2-3   3-4   1 - 2 close to first finger

6. Five Sounds (The Finger Walk)
0 - 1 - 2 - 3 - 4 - 3 - 2 - 1 - 0

> 2nd finger can be played two ways. Try both!

On any one string   Stretch that Pinky!!

INDIAN CHANT

> means to start the sound louder.

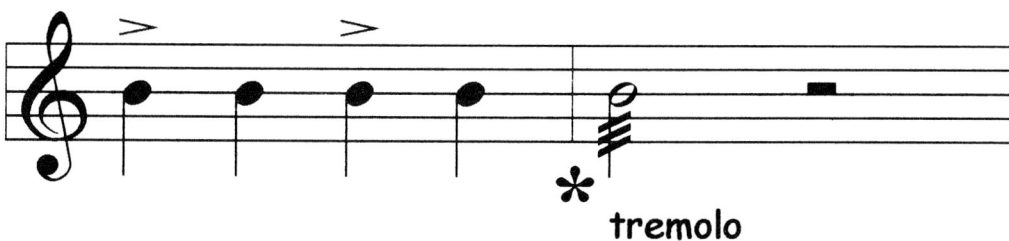

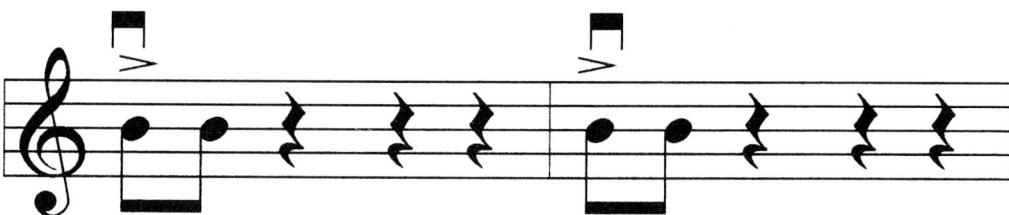

* tremolo

* Try a "tremolo"--a very fast down and up bow at the tip.

"Slurs" make a "Biking Song"

1st--Practice each line over and over.
2nd--Play through as a piece starting on open "D".

Level I

*

0   1   1   0

Keep trying

Until it's easy

Level II

D   A   A   D

Level III

0   1   0   1   0   1   2   3   0

Song ends on Open "D".

* A "Slur" means to connect
   the sounds of 2 or more notes
   with one down-bow or one up-bow.

Finding C Sharp (♯) and C Natural (♮)

You know how to find A & B.......

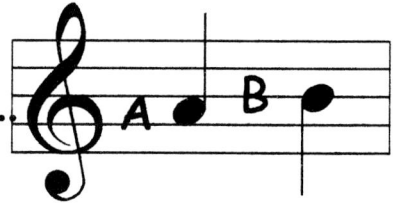

Now find "C" .... on the Third Space.

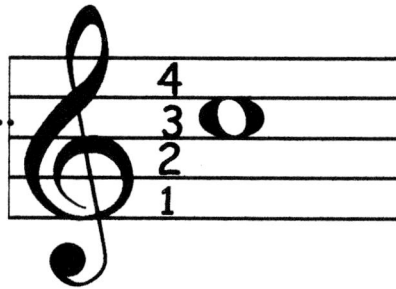

4
3
2
1

Place your 2nd finger close to the 1st finger.

Here is "C♯"

Scoot your 2nd finger away from the 1st finger.

C♯

Here is "C" (♮)

Scoot your 2nd finger back.

C

The Scooter Song

Finding C Sharp and C Natural-2

When is the "C" a Sharp (♯)?

Answer:

The sharp sign (♯)
in the 3rd space
means all C's
will become C ♯'s.

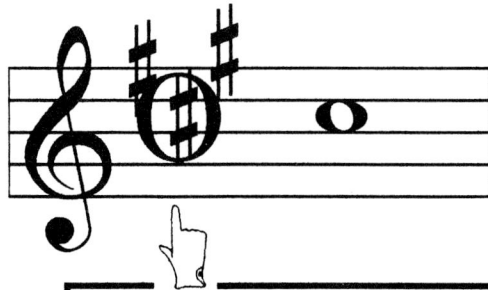

Meet the key signature

Keep Your Eyes on the Key Signature!

1.

2.

3.

4.

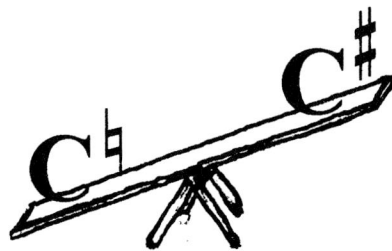

5. "The See-Saw Song"

Hey! This is Work! But Fun!!

Finding C Sharp and C Natural-1

THE TRAINS--G, D, & A Strings

All Fingers Aboard!

1
2
3
4

"All Aboard!"

The next open string may be plucked (pizz.) with the left hand 4th finger.

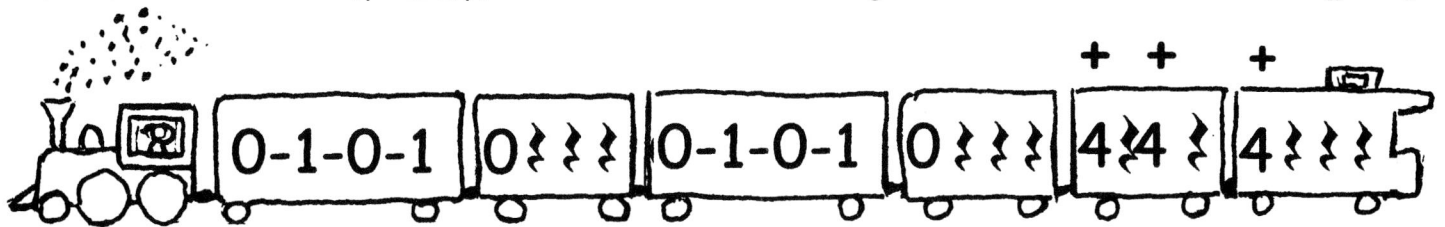

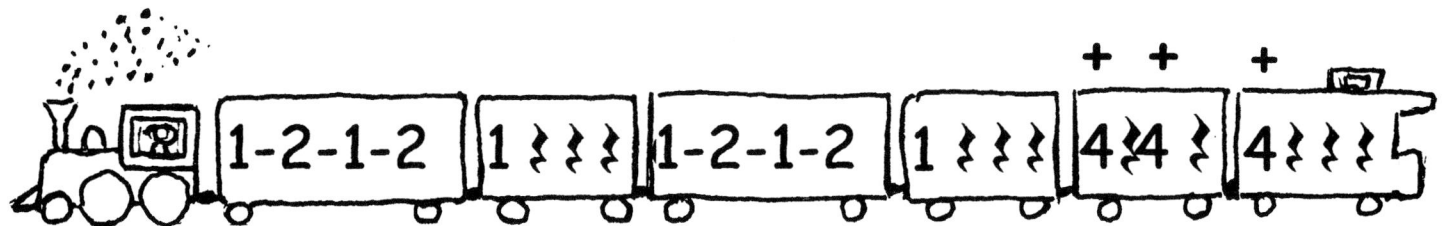

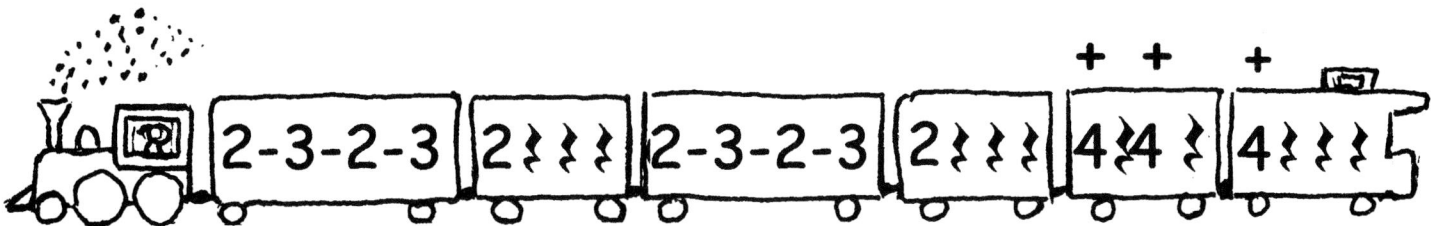

				+ +	+
0-1-0-1	0 𝄾𝄾𝄾	0-1-0-1	0 𝄾𝄾𝄾	4 4 𝄾	4 𝄾𝄾𝄾

				+ +	+
1-2-1-2	1 𝄾𝄾𝄾	1-2-1-2	1 𝄾𝄾𝄾	4 4 𝄾	4 𝄾𝄾𝄾

				+ +	+
2-3-2-3	2 𝄾𝄾𝄾	2-3-2-3	2 𝄾𝄾𝄾	4 4 𝄾	4 𝄾𝄾𝄾

Choose another string & do it again.

Trains3

Tune Snatches
with Finger Numbers

"D" = D string   "A" = A string

— = 2 beat sound = ♩   —— = 4 beat sound = o

Merrily We Roll Along

any string

open
2-1-0-1- | 2-2-2— | 1-1-1— | 2-2-2—

2-1-0-1- | 2-2-2— | 1-1-2-1- | 0——

Twinkle, Twinkle Little Star

D A   A   D
0-0-0-0 | 1-1-0— | 3-3-2-2 | 1-1-0—

Song of Joy

D   A A D   D
2-2-3-0 | 0-3-2-1 | 0-0-1-2 | 2-1-1—

D   A   D
2-2-3-0 | 0-3-2-1 | 0-0-1-2 | 1-0-0—

Tune Snatches--finger #s

A Different "C"

B & C become Friends
1st & 2nd are close together

$\frac{4}{4}$ A A A A | B B B B | C C C C | D D D D

$\frac{4}{4}$ D D D D | C C C C | B B B B | A A A A

$\frac{3}{4}$ A A A | C C C | B B B | D D D

$\frac{2}{4}$ A A | B B | C C | D D | B B | C C

"C" = "C♮"

A B C

A B C#

A Sad Song

A B C — | A B C — | A B C D | C B A —

A Happy Song

A B C# — | A B C# — | A B C#D | C#B A —

A Different C

Stop! Look! Listen!

Look! Key Signature

Ma-ry had a   lit-tle lamb.

Ted-dy had a   lit-tle bird.

Hot Cross Buns, Hot Cross Buns,

Cold Cross Buns, Cold Cross Buns!

Key signature watch

ISBN 1-893178-00-5

9 781893 178007